A View from the Pit

A View from the Pit

(30 Years of Opera Theater in Mid-America)

BY
RUSSELL PATTERSON

Illustrated by Don Carlton
Introduction by Arthur S. Brisbane

ON THE 30TH ANNIVERSARY OF
THE LYRIC OPERA OF KANSAS CITY

(AN ONGOING EXPERIMENT)

THE LOWELL PRESS / KANSAS CITY

FIRST EDITION
Copyright © 1987 by Russell Patterson
Library of Congress Catalog Card Number 87-046008
ISBN 0-932845-25-8

All rights reserved. No part of this book may be reproduced,
stored in a retrieval system, or transmitted in any form or by any
means, electronic, mechanical, photocopying, recording or otherwise
without the prior written permission of the publisher.
Printed in the United States of America by The Lowell Press, Inc.
Kansas City, Missouri.

This chronicle of the past 30 years of one company's attempt to involve a broad segment of the people of its community and surrounding region in such a multifaceted art form as opera-theater is only possible because so many of those people kept the dream alive and growing for these past three decades.

A list of those generous and supportive individuals (many of whom have been and are personal friends as well as colleagues) would take more space than this entire chronicle. I hope it will be read by many of them with the knowledge that my association with them has been, and continues to be, a most joyful part of my life. I hope the Lyric Opera has added to their lives even a small portion of what it has to mine.

RUSSELL PATTERSON
(Rolf Petrach)

CONTENTS

PREFACE ix
INTRODUCTION BY ARTHUR S. BRISBANE xiii
FOREWORD xvii
PRELUDE xix
EXPOSITION 1

1. Help Stamp Out Opera! 3
2. Cueing the Lamppost 9
3. Serving the Devil 15
4. Lights or Dark Coffee? 17
5. At Home with Opera 21
6. SRO—The Kitchen Sink? 23
7. Out of the Pit 27
8. Show Me Your Form! 31
9. A Week That "Rocked" the Opera 35
10. Weren't You Rolf Petrach? 39

DEVELOPMENT 43

11. Moving Uptown 45
12. To Downtown 49
13. And Out-of-Town 53
14. Ford-Funds-Feds 57
15. Co-Opera 65

RECAPITULATION 71

16. Festival Fun and Games 73
17. Repertoire—Who Done It!. 77
18. Quo Vadis—Auf English 85

AFTERWORD 92

PREFACE

The Americanization of Opera
(A Dream Fulfilled)

Leonard Bernstein, defining the nature of opera on the popular "Omnibus" program, described it as "theater with the added dimension of music." Russell Patterson, General Director of the Lyric Opera of Kansas City and one of its founding principals, agreed. "When we formed the Lyric, we called it The Kansas City Lyric Theater. We wanted a place for those who love theater and those who love music. They discovered that opera was fun—not a cultural castor oil." In the 29 seasons it has been performing, the Lyric has done just that: built its own audience of opera lovers and music theater fans throughout the region.

Association with the Bavarian State Opera had convinced Patterson that opera sung in the language of the audience was the only way it could become a popular art form. "To be understood and enjoyed, there must be a sense of involvement and participation, not just observation." While in

Europe, he became aware that opera companies there were filled with young American singers unable to develop their art in their own country, where the major companies used only experienced European singers and regional opera companies were too few to offer satisfactory opportunities to the involuntary expatriates.

When Patterson returned from his European studies and subsequent conducting experience in Germany and the Netherlands, he resolved to establish a platform for American artists and opera for American audiences. He chose Kansas City, where he had played with the Philharmonic and taught at the Conservatory of Music. "It had the three necessary ingredients," Patterson said. "A professional orchestra, a top-level music school, and a vital, growing environment. Besides, I had fallen in love with the city."

When the Lyric was finally established and was gaining national acclaim, Patterson implemented the third principle on which he had worked to establish his company: the performance of American works. "It is essential that our own works be performed. We were one of the few places in the country doing American opera in the early sixties. Now it is a trend, and I feel an important one. If our own operas aren't produced and appreciated, the art form will die and with it a portion of our national cultural identity. We are fortunate to have an audience in Kansas City willing to hear, experience, and enjoy new things." The Lyric Opera of Kansas City has produced and recorded more American opera than any other standard repertory company, a record Patterson revels in as an indication of the Lyric Opera's contribution to the development of opera in America and the acceptance of it as an indigenous art form. The dream of the Americanization of opera is continuing to be fulfilled.

          (From the *Kansas City Magazine*)

INTRODUCTION

I always thought talent was crucial in the opera. Then Russell Patterson asked me to be in one.

"Would you perform in *Fidelio?*" he said.

I blushed. It had been years since anyone asked me to sing. And, although my real ambition had been (and still is) to sing the national anthem at Royals Stadium, I agreed in an instant. I assumed I would have a medium-sized part, since the leads were probably all taken by professionals.

Imagine my surprise the first day of rehearsal, when they handed me my costume and, before I could clear my throat, someone slapped a swatch of masking tape over my mouth and said, "You are a supernumerary, see if it fits."

The costume fit fine, but the tape was tight.

As I shuffled over to the dressing room, I turned the word over in my mind. Supernumerary, supernumerary ... an extra in the opera. They put all those syllables in there as a consolation, I supposed, but there is no consoling a man with his face taped shut. Especially once he gets a look in the mirror.

My costume, I had to admit, was excellent. I was to be some sort of Prussian military figure, it seemed. Great blue and tan color guard outfit, with shiny boots to stomp around in. And stomp I did, reveling in my character. So engrossed was I, in my stomping around the dressing room, that at first I failed to note a rather large group of other people also flailing around in mock characterizations: clerics baptizing infants, merchants peddling their wares, country squires polishing their buttons. All with their faces taped shut.

They were supers, every one.

What a marvelous time we had, after we noticed each other. We were a corps, not just a bunch of folks without parts. We had esprit! Ripping the tape from our mouths, we introduced ourselves.

Oh, and we supers were good when our moment came. Fodder in the Lyric cannon, we performed as the true professionals most of us weren't. On stage, we were luminous—which is to say, nobody fell down. Backstage, we were fastidious, sewing our costumes at the slightest sign of a tear, buffing our makeup, adjusting our tape . . .

Let it be said, indeed, that in the finest tradition of the Lyric Opera—after 30 years, one can speak of tradition—the supers of *Fidelio* came through. Somebody has to be the crowd in a crowd scene.

It may not take talent to look like a crowd, but it does take enthusiasm. That's what I learned about the opera from

Russell. The Lyric, nearly 30 years under his direction, has thrived not just on the talent of its stars but on the enthusiasm of its extras.

By extras, you understand, I don't simply refer to supernumeraries. An equally spirited corps of supporters working offstage has transformed the Lyric from a noble experiment to an established institution, a prominent feature of the Kansas City landscape.

Not bad for a group of folks who have had some of the mishaps you'll read about in Russell's engaging memoir here. Not bad at all.

ARTHUR S. BRISBANE
Washington, D.C.

FOREWORD

After more than a quarter century of speaking to service clubs, women's leagues, opera guilds, church socials, study clubs, trade conventions, and almost any gathering of laymen interested in the arts, I have found that almost without exception those in attendance want to feel a sense of involvement, participation, and understanding of the wonderful human elements which so often make those all-too-unforgettable moments of live performance memorable.

In my attempts at what my good friend and colleague Richard Gaddes (founder and for many years General Director of the Opera Theatre of Saint Louis), once called the "de-mystification" of opera, I have often told some of those anecdotes based on the larger-than-life true happenings which "insiders" of all opera, ballet, and theater companies exchange. I also usually reveal some of the extraordinary attempts made by a dedicated (and zealous, to say the least) group of opera theater enthusiasts to "sell" their art form to a "Show-Me" potential audience.

As the seasons rolled by, the Lyric's small stock of legends grew as did, I am afraid, the length of my talks including them.

Invariably, after one of those perhaps overly incident-laden talks, I have been beseeched to "write down your story, especially those funny things that happened on the way to getting your opera company started." Those requests, I suspect, often came from friends of many years standing who have heard them too many times and wish I had some newer material. Maybe they are right!

So, in response to those always curious and deeply appreciated supporters of opera theater in general (and particularly the Lyric Opera of Kansas City during the past 30 years), I am finally doing it—if for no other reason than I won't have to keep telling the story, at least up to this point.

PRELUDE

I'm not really certain when this obsession with opera-theater began or whom to blame for inflicting me with it. So many people and situations have to share the blame, starting perhaps with a drummer in Sharkey Bonanno's Bunch ("Music with a Peel") who sent a young Dixieland trumpet player to his first opera, even though the black drummer wasn't allowed to attend in New Orleans at that time. Then there was Walter Herbert who allowed me to carry his briefcase on occasion and sing in a chorus which pronounced Verdi or Wagner with a French accent. I probably still hold a dubious record of some sort for a *Tristan und Isolde* production there: singing chorus in act 1, playing offstage horn calls in act 2, and cueing the English horn in act 3—all in the same performance!

Then, as a horn player, student, and general nuisance, I got mixed up with Boris Goldovsky's incredibly gifted New England Opera Theater group which involved not only Boris and that phenomenon Sarah Caldwell but also such young artists as Phyllis Curtin, Eunice Alberts, David Lloyd, Mack

Morgan, Jimmy Pease, and "Roz" Elias. With Nat Merrill as technical director, Phil de Rosier as set designer, and the costuming of Leo van Witzen, one could hardly stop the infection from spreading.

The final contamination occurred in Europe where naturally one heard *Di Cantarini di Nurenburger* in Milano and *Das Macht der Schicksal* in Munich sung (even in the early '50s) by a mixture of locals and operatic expatriates from the United States who, while well trained, were handicapped by the lack of opportunity for onstage experience with the few major houses in their own country. Already influenced by Boris Goldovsky's beliefs in opera as theater as well as Lenny Bernstein's teaching that "opera should be theater with the added dimension of music," I realized that hearing "Wie eiskalt ist dein händchen" meant more to the audience leaning on the rail of the Staatsoper in Munich than "Che gelida manina" would. Could there ever be an involvement by audiences in Mid-America with this multifaceted art form, so long accepted throughout Europe? Many operatic forums throughout the United States and Canada are now involving audiences in ever-growing numbers. This, then, is a story about some of the things that happened on the way to our forum, the Lyric Opera of Kansas City.

EXPOSITION

Help Stamp Out Opera!

As late as the 1950s, professional opera in the United States consisted mainly of The Metropolitan Opera (in New York as well as on tour), the San Francisco Opera, Lyric Opera of Chicago, and no more than a score of other companies, mostly in older cities which periodically imported stars from the Met, rented scenery and costumes from one or two collections, and stirred together these elements with the local symphony and choral group. The result often was "instant opera" consisting of periods of great singing, moments of good individual characterization, and hours of mediocre theater. The one notable exception to that was at the old City Center in New York where (thanks to the Ford Foundation) some new operas were being underwritten and the roster of artists allowed for American singers, a few of whom trekked out to Central City for a month in the summer.

In most of our country, especially west of the Mississippi River, opera was thought of in Maggie and Jiggs cartoon terms: a 300-pound soprano in horned helmet shouting at a

98-pound tenor in a language nobody understood, moving off their predetermined marks occasionally to embrace or die, while a mostly stationary choral society struggled through words they didn't understand and wondered (with the audience) what was going to happen next. For this, a man, already drained from a hard day at the office, was forced into evening clothes and dragged by his wife to the local concert hall, where he could be seen having a much-deserved drink at the all-too-brief intermissions! No wonder "opera" was a thing to be avoided, even in locations where symphony orchestras flourished and the local theater and dance companies were "Americanized" enough to do more than Shakespeare or *Swan Lake!*

In this atmosphere, it seemed one had not only to produce opera-theater in a manner attractive to a potential audience which had not grown up surrounded by the traditions of Europe but one also had to "sell" the idea of actually enjoying an evening of musical theater.

We even went so far as to name our enterprise The Kansas City Lyric Theater (thus avoiding the dreaded term, *op-rah*) and embarked on a rather unusual, for then, promotion of the concept. Bumper stickers proclaiming "Help Stamp Out Opera!" had to be backed up with posters of a truly corpulent "Valkyrie" captioned: "If this is what you are expecting, have we got a surprise for you!" Then came the numerous visits to Rotary, Lions, and Kiwanis clubs with an attractive Musetta wearing a split skirt for her tabletop waltz scene. Suddenly some of those Jiggs woke up to the fact that opera-theater wasn't all unintelligible—maybe they would even urge their Maggies to get involved with this thing!

Not that we weren't seriously dedicated to the art form. As a matter of fact, the original declaration of the company's credo sounded pompous even to our ears. The five articles of faith adopted by the group of founding board members were:

We believe there exists in every metropolitan center of the United States a substantial—and largely untapped—public for professional opera-theater;

We believe this public may best be reached through the establishment of resident repertory companies with a regional scope, adequately rehearsed and performing in the language of the audience;

We believe there is a wealth of young singing and acting talent in this country which, while well trained, is presently handicapped by lack of opportunity for onstage experience in a sufficient variety of roles;

We are convinced that a nationwide network of such companies would go far toward correcting that lack;

Finally, it is our opinion that there can never be a truly indigenous American opera until the country first develops its own corps of conductors, stage directors, and performing artists capable of handling the work of American composers and librettists—because foreigners, however gifted, are not so equipped.

These lofty principles and goals were supported enthusiastically by a small and unlikely combination of music and theater lovers, led by Henry C. Haskell (a playwright, newspaper editor, and true believer in opera-theater) and Mike Berbiglia (a leading purveyor of spirits who at first only accepted Mozart because that genius composed most of his operas in Italian!). Mike finally admitted to liking opera-theater in English and, as chairman of the board, opened the doors of arriving cars and greeted each patron with heartfelt warmth at virtually every performance those first few years.

That initial board of directors, numbering less than a dozen, was composed of friends of Haskell and Berbiglia and included donated legal advice by Nathan Stark (a vice president of Hallmark Cards) and comptroller services by Lyle Kennedy (business manager of the Conservatory of Music and the original catalyst for getting Haskell and Berbiglia together). We were an inexperienced, unlikely collection of dreamers setting sail in the face of those either indifferent to opera per se or in rare cases opera buffs who 1) did at least listen to Met broadcasts, 2) had collected all the recordings of Caruso, 3) were conditioned to opera in the grand manner, and 4) were, of course, instinctively suspicious of any homegrown enterprise. To them opera had to be done lavishly or not at all and preferably should come from New York, if not Europe—otherwise, how could it be called professional? We foresaw these problems. We did not foresee the challenges facing us in our first home, the Rockhill Theatre.

Cueing the Lamppost

A less likely home for what Americans had come to regard as one of the more sumptuous of the performing arts would have been hard to find. The Rockhill, a 40-year-old motion picture theater being used to screen foreign and domestic art films, stood with its inconspicuous entrance sandwiched between an alley and a storefront in a minor Southside shopping center. Its tiny lobby opened into an exceedingly plain auditorium which could seat only 762 customers—but it did possess excellent acoustics and sight lines. An orchestra pit could be improvised and the dressing rooms, though primitive, just might do. But there was one major difficulty about which virtually nothing could be done—the stage was 13 feet deep with no wing-space and no flyloft!

Harassed stage directors had to plot their blockings with the precision of an army drill, scenic designers had to invent perspectives, and adequate lighting required a triumph of ingenuity. Since, in this somewhat limited space, artists had to interact closely and even "die" cautiously (or else risk falling into the orchestra pit), a few noteworthy improvisations occurred. For example, the firing squad in *Tosca* was instructed to carefully aim upstage of Cavaradossi, lest the discharge of wadding from blank ammunition at such close range would make the performance a truly *verismo* one!

In an effort to remain within the all-too-limited budget for special effects (and at the request of one member of the firing squad who objected to discharging any kind of weapon), the stage manager consistently loaded only three of the four rifles utilized. Naturally, that one soldier, aware of his unloaded weapon, aimed his rifle virtually under the nose of the tenor. During a performance toward the end of the season, it was discovered that we were running out of blank shells so, in democratic fashion, the firing squad (with the exception of the tardy conscientious objector) drew lots for the task of firing the final round. They, of course, selected the unknowing fellow in jest but failed to inform the stage manager or anyone else in the cast.

As the officer approached with a blindfold, which the courageous leading tenor dramatically declined, he informed the doomed man of the loaded rifle situation. One can scarcely blame an artist who placed his career (and perhaps even his life) before realistic drama, but I have never again witnessed a Cavaradossi fall immediately *before* the volley!

To make matters worse, the, by now, completely flustered rifleman was shaking so violently that his bayonet fell from the quivering rifle and became embedded in the stage floor.

Only the dedicated singing actress portraying Tosca that night could have ignored that gleaming protrusion while being chased by Spoletta and Sciarone—finally seizing it to hold her pursuers at bay and dropping it as she flung herself from the parapet of Castel Sant Angelo. No, neither she nor the bayonet reappeared in view of the audience.

The absence of wing-space meant that before entering the pit, I had to confirm with the stage manager our readiness to start any act by long distance. He (or she) would call an OK from stage level to the conductor waiting at the pit entrance. Before the final act of *The Force of Destiny* (which has an orchestral introduction of only 16 measures in a fast tempo) I, after waiting for what seemed an interminable interval, called to the stage manager, "Is it OK to go?" Unfortunately, that pressured coordinator was simultaneously being asked by a crew member, "Is it OK to place the benches on their marks?" Upon hearing the reply "OK!" (addressed to the stagehand), I strode into the pit, gave the orchestra a bow, and plunged into that 16-measure introduction, at the end of which the curtain did not move! The ensuing ominous silence was broken only by my under-the-breath questions concerning the ancestry of the curtain hands, who had obviously missed their cue. Undaunted, I magnaminously gave them a second chance by repeating the 16 measures, by which time the still-not-ready stage manager cued the curtain with crossed fingers. Imagine the surprise registered by the now-wide-awake audience as well as myself (not to mention the astonished stagehand caught stage center with bench in hand)! As he walked to the safe obscurity of offstage right, he passed in front of a kneeling Leonora pleading the English equivalent of "Pace, Mio Dio!" My sentiments exactly!

That same *Forza* production indirectly enhanced my reputation as a thorough, if somewhat overly meticulous, conductor in some opera circles. Since we needed a smoke machine for the battle scenes in *Forza* (a financial extravagance reluctantly agreed to by our comptroller), I suggested we justify this equipment rental by utilizing it to create fog for the opening of act 3 of *La Bohème*. Due to a most efficient air conditioner return vent over the stage, the crew seemed unable to have sufficient fog lingering on the ground as the curtain rose on that scene.

General directors of opera companies (especially if they are conductors or stage directors who tend to get into every detail of a production) more often than not get what they request, if not always what they deserve, from efficient stage crews. Our excellent master carpenter and his special effects staff assured me there would be plenty of fog for the final performance of the season—and there was! After turning off the air conditioner and pumping the stage full of fog during the intermission, even the crew was surprised by the wave of dense fog which engulfed the orchestra pit and first several rows of the audience upon opening the curtain. The orchestra valiantly struggled to read the music, the audience coughed more than the truly ill Mimi waiting in the wings, and I wished for a lighted baton to cleave through the thick atmosphere.

Suddenly we had arrived at the first entrance of the gendarme replying to the choked cries of the women's chorus at the hazy gates of Paris. I threw a most obvious cue to the tall figure looming out of the mist, only to hear his voice coming from another spot where he was wandering through the fog. I had cued the lamppost!

Several weeks later I was in New York and stopped by to pay my respects to John Gutman (assistant manager of the Metropolitan Opera) who, upon seeing me, burst into laughter and said, "Russell, I have often heard that you never miss giving an entrance to your artists, but really! Cueing even the lamppost?" I could only reply that we were really involving the audience, even if we had to resort to fog to do so.

Serving the Devil

We were involving some members of the community in more ways than at our actual performances. Due to the extremely limited dressing room space (of course, not air conditioned for Kansas City in September), some of our artists preferred to makeup at their more comfortable apartments, especially if rather elaborate detail was required for their roles. One such young bass-baritone, who made his professional debut with our fledgling company on his way to the roster of the Met, was the Mephistopheles in full makeup that ran out of gas on his way to the theater. Only after calmly filling his gas tank did he taunt the amazed collection of station attendants with "Haven't you fellows ever served the Devil before?"

On a somewhat higher end of the scale there was the most helpful group of nuns who, upon being asked to contribute their discarded habits to help in costuming of the Te Deum for *Tosca,* explained that consecrated habits had to be destroyed but helped us duplicate other authentically styled ones. In gratitude for their generosity, they came as guests of the company for opening night. While chatting with their similarly clad stage counterparts from the chorus by the stage door, they were more than somewhat astonished to see one of their group affectionately patted on the derriere by one of the male cast members. He had mistaken her for a friend in the ensemble. Imagine *his* feelings when the Mother Superior turned on his "nice show, kid" compliment with a look of pleasure and forgiveness!

Those same nuns' costumes helped publicize the company in other ways. There being no artists' canteen or waiting area (other than the infamous stage door alley even on rainy nights) and having an adjacent small tavern whose owner agreed to pipe in the sound from the theater, we allowed our artists to be on call there in costume. The regular bar patrons took this pretty much in stride, but when a newcomer looked disapprovingly at what he took to be a nun downing a beer and smoking in public, the chorister in question paused from her libation long enough to genuflect and pronounce "Bless you my son and cast no stones in this house of glasses."

Bill's Tavern became such a favorite watering hole for our artists, staff, and even board members before, during and after performances that Bill actually had Mario Lanza recordings mixed in with Elvis Presley on his juke box. That's also getting involved.

Lights or Dark Coffee?

Getting lay persons involved (especially those ladies who eventually form women's leagues that are an integral part of the support structure of any arts organization) usually requires allowing them to exercise two basic desires: an outlet for artistic talents and a chance to serve coffee, tea, or cocktails. Our Women's Committee (later to become a more formal Women's League) started life as the wives of our board members who not only organized our first, and badly needed, ticket campaign but also stenciled numbers on the auditorium seats (not needed for a movie house) and painted the dressing rooms and backstage area. These women were long on talent and determination but short on the neutral color paint needed for makeup areas. One of them apparently had gallons of excess swimming pool paint. Have you ever tried to blend makeup in a room reflecting aquamarine tones?

We then decided to entrust to them the preparation and serving of coffee in the theater lobby during intermissions. We carefully explained the problems which could be created by a sudden surge of power usage in a poorly wired older theater being asked to accommodate theatrical lighting. You

guessed it! A total blackout of the stage, pit, and aisle lights during that marvelous act 2 finale of *The Marriage of Figaro* when an overeager volunteer plugged in five coffee pots in anticipation of the forthcoming intermission! As our sellouts became more frequent, a separate power line to the concession area was needed—for artistic purposes.

While their wives were inadvertently playing games with the theater's lighting system, it seems that our zealous box office manager was doing the same with our board members' tickets. These die-hard converts to opera-theater held seats for every performance of each production and generally used them every night, only allowing us to resell them when they were out of town or personally at death's door.

One rainy evening, I stuck my head in Bill's Tavern (to await my summons to the pit, of course) where I found half of the Board of Directors apparently downing a few at curtain time. I proceeded to endear myself with these friends (and important supporters) by accusing them of reverting to Jigg-ism under fire (while their loyal Maggies slaved over hot coffee pots in the lobby of the Rockhill Theater). Only then did I learn that these loyal patrons' regular seats had all been resold at an SRO performance, and they were patiently planning to listen to the performance from the tavern while visiting with the artists awaiting their calls to the stage. That lecture cost me several rounds of drinks at the conclusion of that performance, which those "involved gentlemen" insisted was a particularly fluid one!

At Home with Opera

Shortly after our Women's Committee organized that first season ticket campaign, several of our board members, who were active with the Metropolitan Opera National Council and its nationwide guild, suggested the formation of a Lyric Theater Guild. This organization (originally headed by a series of presidents appointed from our board of directors) was not only to help spread knowledge and understanding of opera in general throughout our city and its surrounding region but also to allow greater involvement in support of the Lyric by an ever-growing number of working people unable to attend Women's Committee luncheons or afternoon meetings. This group of highly self-motivated converts to the cause (they referred to themselves as Lyric Nuts) reached out into the community in a much broader way than our small board, limited staff, or even the active Women's Committee could.

At the urging of a few scattered members of the new guild and through the auspices of the University's program in continuing education, I reluctantly offered a 15-week course in the history of opera. To my surprise, that class sold out in a matter of days, and before all those original (and insatiable) guild members let up, we had gone through several other courses in Verdi, Wagner, Mozart, and Richard Strauss.

The guild members then became teachers and spread the word like traveling evangelists, organizing groups throughout the city for "At Home with Opera" evenings, where I originally led discussions on the Lyric's forthcoming productions. When that didn't satisfy their voracious appetites, they developed pairs of research/lectures (like great books clubs) and exchanged programs from home to home, often having parties where everyone came dressed as an operatic character.

Of course, tied in with all the fun of those regular gatherings, the guild not only became a social and educational force for the company but also developed organized trips to other cities, did radiothons and other fund-raising activities, arranged transportation and personal assistance for visiting artists, and supplied us with a large (and enthusiastic) source for "supers" and administrative volunteers. They even bussed merrily along on our tours, like so many college football addicts.

I think, more than in any other way, the Lyric became more than a "cultural castor oil" (good for the city to have in regular doses) or an adjunct to social distinction (a la Maggie and Jiggs) through the image and activities of the guild. They indeed do love the Lyric!

SRO–The Kitchen Sink?

As our 762 auditorium seats (and minuscule balcony of 50 or so more) began to be sold out on a regular basis, we added a few chairs at the back and in the wider aisles. Then our irrepressible Board Chairman Mike Berbiglia came up with the seemingly clever idea of selling my conductor's chair out of the pit. The Rockhill orchestra pit was rather shallow and my 6'1" frame would have obstructed the view from a number of the higher priced seats in the first several rows, so I customarily sat on a stool while conducting. It was decided that Mike would personally remove and sell the stool immediately before the next SRO performance.

As fate would have it, our young Assistant Conductor, Rick Fanning (now a highly respected coach in Europe), had been in the pit for a *Barber of Seville* performance two nights earlier and had removed my stool. A night later I discovered the stool missing when I was forced to conduct the seemingly endless act 1 of *Madame Butterfly* in a half-crouched position. Between acts that night, I informed Maestro Fanning that if I ever found my chair missing under

similar circumstances, he would be fired on the spot!

On the following eventful night, Rick was sitting at the harpsichord awaiting my entrance when a person, unknown to him, of course, suddenly reached over the orchestra pit railing and started to remove my chair. Heeding my threats to his livelihood, Rick raced forth and seized the legs of the chair, resulting in a tug-of-war in front of a packed house between the Chairman of the Board and the Assistant Conductor. Hissing "Let go! Russell knows all about this!" Mike's Italian fervor and determination won the tug-of-war. Rick rushed to meet me at the pit entrance crying: "Don't blame me, but some nut just stole your chair!" The final result of this clever publicity stunt (which was dutifully recorded in the local press) was that it produced a brush with the city's fire marshal, effectively ending the addition of chairs in the auditorium.

We did subsequently sell space in the tiny office of the theater manager which overlooked the stage and contained a sink—which thereby allowed us to proclaim we had even sold "the kitchen sink!" But somehow that didn't match the unforgettable sight of the "Great Chair-Tug-of-War"!

Out of the Pit

The Lyric Opera of Kansas City has always been a family organization. Not only was the original board a source of advice to me, consulted regularly on general policies while leaving all purely artistic decisions to the General Artistic Director but the relationship has also proved remarkably harmonious, primarily because both parties have remained faithful to the statement of principles adopted at the Lyric's inception.

So have the various production, administrative, and support elements grown to feel the Lyric is their family. Our stage crew takes pride in their contributions (from developing 4-fold flat units in order to squeeze more elaborate scenery through undersized loading doors onto postage-stamp stages, to self-motivated design of acoustical ceilings and special stands for touring, to makeshift pits). The orchestra (originally colleagues from the old Philharmonic and now the Kansas City Symphony) has always gone far beyond the call of duty—maybe even a little *too* far when asked, as evidenced by the following episode.

In the early days of the Lyric, we were limited to one full dress rehearsal with the orchestra and, in order to save time, I often talked through spots which hadn't been cleared up in the previous *sitzprobe* (or purely musical rehearsals) with soloists and orchestra. On one such occasion, I turned to our principal horn (a longtime colleague who is not only a talented and experienced performer with the love of opera and its traditions that only an Italian musician inherits but one who also is known to possess a sense of humor). He had asked about a certain "echo" passage in *Gianni Schicchi.* The moment in question comes as Schicchi warns the relatives of the deceased, wealthy Donati of what they stand to lose if a false will is discovered by the authorities. As he waves his "amputated" fingers in the air, Schicchi intones "Let us contemplate Florence!" An "echo" of that freely interpreted melody is to follow from the solo horn.

Since I don't normally conduct the singer in his brief cadenza, I decided to let the horn player copy the singer's tempo and style. "Just repeat what he does" were my fateful instructions. At the proper moment of what, thank God, was a smoothly flowing dress rehearsal, the horn player stood and *sang* "Let us contemplate Florence" (and in more accurate pitch and rhythm than the original artist he was answering). It is extremely difficult to fire anyone who follows your instructions to the actual letter. Also, Frank was (and still is) the orchestra's personnel manager!

We utilized a somewhat unorthodox seating arrangement in the cramped Rockhill pit by placing the horns at one end of the pit and the other brasses opposite them. The stereo effect created by this arrangement received plaudits from our front-row season ticket holders since they did not experience Vesuvius erupting at every fortissimo brass entrance. Little did these faithful patrons realize my true motive for this seating arrangement. I was aware that this same horn player knew more jokes than anyone (other than perhaps our timpanist), and while he personally seldom missed a musical entrance, I couldn't take the chance of having an entire brass section convulsed with laughter over the whispered critique of some not-so-Italianate tenor by that witty and outspoken principal horn just as *La Bohème* was coming to its final chords. I guess involvement does have its limit!

Show Me Your Form!

Informal social activities surround most performing arts organizations at summer festivals (or winter if in Florida, the Southwest, or southern California). These groups often have picnics and ad hoc golf or tennis activities. We at the Lyric, however, do seem to be into that sort of thing to a greater degree than most, probably again due to the family atmosphere created by close relationships which have developed over the years among our board, guild, staff, and artists. Contrary to a popular misconception (still circulating in some New York talent agencies), these activities do not affect casting decisions, staff engagements, or selection of board members.

Some years ago, under the leadership of an extremely active member of our board who owned a wonderful farm (complete with tennis court, a barn with billiards, pool, and other indoor sporting equipment as well as volleyball, softball, and touch football areas in adjacent pastures), we started having entire company sports picnics. Out of these record-breaking contests (which featured such heartbreaking sagas as Katy Christenson's "19 hitter" which was lost in the final inning when a fastidious violinist refused to pick up the softball just because it had fallen into a fresh cowpie) grew the idea for an ongoing organization: the KCLTLTA, the Kansas City Lyric Theater Lawn Tennis Association. Sally (the above-mentioned board member) designed a logo which was printed on tennis shirts for the entire company and a large trophy was displayed in the lobby of the theater on which each season's winners were listed. The annual invitational tournament (which was open to all members of the company, guild, women's league, board, etc.) grew to the point where we took over half of Woodside Racquet Club for a weekend each season—and that was for the finals and trophy awards party!

Being pressured by members of the board and support groups to re-engage certain artists because of their tennis skills was bad enough, but the news spread (as it always does in this business). While holding our periodic auditions in New York, I began to notice normally reserved artists posing in the most unusual positions. During a break in the schedule of applicants, I stepped out of the hall to see if anyone was waiting, only to discover two of our tennis playing artists suggesting to their colleagues that if the applicants could only convince me by their stage deportment that they were tennis players, I would most certainly engage them! Not true! They had to sing pretty well also.

It is also not true that I engaged two production staff people because they go to Royals baseball games with me. It *is* true that I try to avoid conflicts with Royals and Chiefs games in scheduling rehearsals. During the 1985 playoffs and World Series we announced the scores from the stage between acts only because we wanted to get the audience back from a transistor-radio-filled lobby, to make sure no artist missed the act curtain, and to keep the crew busy changing scenery. In order to protect our artists from themselves (since one soprano lost her voice screaming at a Chiefs-Raiders football game) we now insist that any board member who invites artists to Sunday games will be held responsible for their Monday night's vocal condition!

A Week That "Rocked" the Opera

Just as the initial recording of *Jesus Christ Superstar* was beginning to take the U.S. by storm, we were determined to be the first American opera company to present this then still somewhat controversial work. We were aware that the stage rights (and subsequent film rights) had been taken by a New York producer but arranged (through an independent agent) to present the work in a semi-concert format utilizing only theatrical lighting and contemporary costuming to create what atmosphere we could in a 10,000-seat arena. With the Lyric Opera chorus and orchestra, soloists from the agent's roster, and the New Heavenly Blue led by Chris Brubeck engaged, we enthusiastically sold over 15,000 single tickets through several box office outlets with, of course, no record of who purchased them. We couldn't cancel and refund if we wanted to.

We were eagerly preparing to begin a five-day rehearsal period when the producing agent arrived with *one* singer (his wife who was scheduled to do the role of Mary Magdalen), a score but no orchestra parts, and the news that the other scheduled soloists (fearing the rumor of an injunction) would not be arriving to appear with us. An emergency retreat to Sally's farm (of KCLTLTA fame) where the New Heavenly Blue was rehearsing in the barn, brought us together with the famous photographer David Douglas Duncan, who was visiting his native city before leaving to do a story on the Kremlin for *Life Magazine*.

David, whose sense for the dramatic in life is equaled by his personal religious convictions, was moved by the disappointment displayed by the young musicians, who themselves were deeply committed to the project. That was true also of the young people in our chorus, who volunteered to cover some of the supporting roles now vacant. Since we had the soprano for the role of Mary, could get a gifted replacement for the combined roles of Herod and Pontius Pilate from New York, and one of the vocalists from the rock group was willing to tackle the part of Judas; we were left with the problems of 1) having no orchestral parts, 2) being down to four days to reassemble our forces, and 3) locating someone who could learn (and sing) the crucial part of Jesus Christ!

The group all felt that Chris Brown (the golden-bearded, soft-spoken guitarist of the New Heavenly Blue) could fill in, since he had been doing so at rehearsals. Chris, however, was reluctant to publicly portray the Savior until David Duncan (after hours of contemplation and discussion while strolling around the farm) persuaded him to do so. Duncan was convinced that the project had taken on a significance beyond its original idea and had persuaded the editors of *Life Magazine* to replace the Kremlin story with one on the various religious movements among young people throughout the country, including the reaction to the popularity of *Jesus Christ Superstar*. *Life* sent out a writer to do the story (who managed to bring several of David's cameras, already packed for shipment to Russia).

During the remaining 48 hours prior to our final rehearsals on the day of the performances, we all stayed awake (fueled by gallons of coffee in Sally's barn) preparing makeshift orchestra parts and copying them. I think we all felt a little like Mozart's copyists on the eve of the premiere of *The Marriage of Figaro* (except that we were aware that virtually everyone in our audience would be more than familiar with what we would be presenting).

During the day of hectic rehearsals at the Municipal Auditorium Arena, it suddenly dawned on me that we would have a problem vacating 10,000 people at the first performance and ushering in the second show crowd with only 30 minutes between performances (a problem we never have to face at the opera). I suggested doing a reprise of the title song at the end of the concert to get the audience on their feet and moving. As it turned out, quite another interpretation was given this idea by the audience and to a degree by the performers. Instead of ending quietly with John 19:40, the reprise of "Superstar" created a mood of resurrection. To this day, I believe, David Duncan feels that decision was divinely inspired.

We rehearsed until 6:00 P.M. and then had to open the doors for the 7:00 first show (the second was scheduled for 9:00), so David and I slipped out for a quick milkshake, only to be confronted by a group of protesters carrying signs attacking the production. At David's insistence, I asked the leader of this group of young religious fanatics why they were protesting. He replied, "This tells the story of the crucifixion, not the resurrection!" For some reason (David still says divine intervention), I blurted out "Oh no! We end it with the resurrection! Be our guests at the second show if you don't believe me!" They all stayed around, dubiously entered for the second show, and ended up as part of the standing ovation (even asking for autographs from the totally exhausted Chris Brown and other cast members).

David Duncan (who seemingly never gets exhausted) was, of course, taking photographs of all this chaos, and when his cover article appeared in *Life,* we found ourselves perhaps more notorious than we had envisioned.

Weren't You Rolf Petrach?

During those first years of the Lyric as the company grew steadily, if not spectacularly, at home, we were achieving some fame in national operatic circles. This was due in part to an address I made at the first national meeting of the Central Opera Service, which was reviewed by a delightful young lady named Shirley Fleming (later to be the editor of *Musical America*). From that, I suspect, as well as the fact that there weren't too many opera companies around regularly presenting American works or even showing a commitment to American artists, I was invited to be a consultant to the Ford Foundation, serve on an advisory panel to the National Endowment for the Arts, and attend the first White House Festival of the Arts, which had a bit of notoriety due to the Vietnam War. For whatever reason, the editor of *Opera News,* Frank Merkling, decided it was time to do a profile on that guy out in Mid-America whose company kept acting like opera was a living art form instead of a museum, whose marketing style was as corny as Kansas in August, and yet seemed to be succeeding in an area famous as "Show Me"!

Some years earlier, when I was in Europe initially on a Fulbright Grant and just starting out to be a conductor, my manager there was having little success getting me engagements as Russell Patterson. He suggested using the name Rolf Petrach professionally (an obvious use of initials, which sounded Middle European) since American conductors weren't as acceptable in Germany in 1952 as singers were. My accent was good enough to pass, but the grammar was a disaster. Actually, it all seemed a great idea. I planned eventually to return to the U.S. with a changed name and "Cherman Akzent" anyway, like Frank Valentine of Philadelphia, Pennsylvania, had done by returning from Italy to the previously unattainable Met for a most successful career as Francesco Valentino. I did a few concerts as Rolf Petrach but eventually returned to Kansas City where I could scarcely show up with a new name and fake accent—so Rolf changed careers and became a translator.

We have given good old Rolf Petrach credit for my own English translations in Lyric Opera programs for years. After all, he doesn't sound any more American than Ruth and Thomas Martin, Joe Machlis, or John Gutman, so he was more acceptable to a still prejudiced (and unsuspecting) audience of opera buffs. When Frank Merkling came to Kansas City (covering the premiere of Douglas Moore's last opera, *Carry Nation,* in nearby Lawrence, Kansas), we did the interview for the *Opera News* profile.

Throughout our conversation about the Lyric and its experiences, Frank kept mentioning that "you look familiar, but the name doesn't ring any bells from the past!" Eventually, we discovered that he had heard a concert in a small town in Bavaria (Tegernsee, I believe) conducted by the young Rolf Petrach, a fact he revealed in the *Opera News* article. Once the story was out, I received a few snide remarks from some of my close friends on the Lyric Board on "reverse prejudice," but we have continued to keep Rolf Petrach alive as a translator.

DEVELOPMENT

Moving Uptown

Immediately after the close of the Lyric's tenth anniversary season, a fire gutted the Rockhill Theatre. Standing in the still-smoldering ruins, Henry Haskell, Mike Berbiglia, and I were interviewed by John Haskins, Music Editor of the *Kansas City Star.* John was, of course, accompanied by a photographer from the news department so we naturally expected a three- or four-column story in the paper. Several hours after the interview, I received a call from John saying he couldn't use any of the photographs because we were all smiling–not too appropriate for the tragedy that had befallen the company. We, mistakenly, had assumed that our city fathers would build a long-needed opera house and were smiling at the thought of a full-sized stage, adequately equipped and more conveniently located than the Rockhill.

This, of course, was not the case and with suitable quarters in short supply, the homeless company was relieved to be offered the use of the Uptown Theatre on Broadway, a motion picture theater with 2,000 seats, a pit which could be extended to accommodate a larger orchestra, and better dressing room facilities. Its two major drawbacks were scarcely more wing space than previously available and a loading door 15 feet up the back wall, which necessitated loading scenery through the lobby, down the aisle, and over the orchestra pit onto the stage.

We spent two years at the Uptown where for the first time we could incorporate limited ballet in our productions, causing yet another incident that threatened our family atmosphere. Encouraged by the much larger stage with more freedom of movement, our artists were no longer in danger of imminent collision and sometimes gave slightly over-realistic performances. When our Petruchio in *The Taming of the Shrew* accidentally bounced a metal serving bowl into the orchestra pit, a delegation from the orchestra informed me that they were understandably concerned for the safety of their instruments (as well as their lives), and if anything else fell into the pit, they were leaving immediately. The entire company was notified that henceforth all thrown, dropped, or even tilted objects were to be carefully aimed upstage.

As luck would have it, several nights later we ended the season with a sold-out performance of *Carmen* where, in the crowd-filled scene of act 2, a whirling gypsy dancer caught Carmen's wig with his arm, sending it hurtling into the orchestra pit, much to the surprise of the principal cellist on whose instrument it came to rest. Fortunately, most of the orchestra was concentrating on the rousing climax of the gypsy dance and didn't notice, although the subsequent line of Zuniga ("Carmen, you seem upset!") was followed by audience laughter which drowned out her reply ("Upset? But why?").

Happily, the amused orchestra did not take a walk until it did so with the entire company in 1970 after a second season at the Uptown, when the impossible dream of a downtown showcase suddenly materialized.

To Downtown

Unlike the Rockhill and the Uptown, the Capri Theatre (originally a Masonic hall) had been adapted as a traditional proscenium theater. At last, the Lyric had access to standard backstage facilities. Furthermore, the Capri's flexible auditorium could seat between 1,200 and 1,300—a capacity we needed since we sold out 18 of our 25 performances. For the first three years we subleased the theater from American Multi Cinema (which first developed the multitheater complex and retained the Capri as the corporation's last large road-show house), but by 1974 we came into exclusive possession of the theater under a long-term lease. We entered the theater rental field for other organizations and were able to consolidate our offices there on a year-round basis. Two years later, thanks to a munificent gift from the Enid and Crosby Kemper Foundation, we were able to renovate the stagehouse as well as refurbish the auditorium, lobbies, and backstage areas. For our 20th anniversary, we installed a new computerized lighting system and renamed our home the Lyric Theatre.

One would think that at last we would be settled into smoothly running, uneventful performances with no more incidents. Wrong again!

Our landlord (whom I hasten to add has been and is extremely cooperative) is one of the leading TV channels in the city. When we first took over the theater, they were accustomed to having movies shown in the house and, although their main studios were located directly under the auditorium, paid little attention to scheduling their live shows opposite movie showings. As you might guess, they programmed a "Battle of the Bands" marathon which ran through one of our *La Traviata* performances. Violetta's poignant reading of Germont's letter and her subsequent death scene were accompanied by a thumping louder than any heartbeat imaginable! Naturally, we quickly got together on coordinating our schedules.

Since the theater was located next door to a major fire station, we lived in constant dread of an ill-timed alarm sounding. Only once in almost ten years did an alarm actually go off in midperformance, and that proved to be a perfectly timed cue. In *The Saint of Bleecker Street,* just as the distant wail of sirens is heard to herald the approach of the police, a 4-alarm call sounded. If I hadn't been in the pit at the time, I am sure I would have been accused of turning in that alarm! The station has since been converted into a businesswomen's club.

Having a traditional-style theater with sufficient space allowed us to produce operas with larger forces on stage, including supernumeraries recruited from various groups in the city—with varied results. One memorable mistake was deciding to cast the "unholy thirteen," including Robespierre (in *Andrea Chenier*) entirely from our board of directors. The worst prima donna or *tenore assoluto* would be a pussycat compared to doctors who are on call constantly and must have "covers" three deep every performance. These highly trained and truly life-saving professionals are accustomed to hospital staffs responding to their needs immediately—something a harried costumer, makeup technician, or stage manager cannot do. In addition, nearly all these "supers" wore glasses, which are not allowed on stage in a period piece, and had to cross a curved bridge in semi-darkness. We finally attached a guide rope to the bridge railing so that they could all grope their way across and then returned their glasses so they could see to sign autographs after the performances. They are wonderful supporters of the opera, and I would much rather consult them on medical matters than our stage crew, but we now look elsewhere for more dependable (and less demanding) "supers."

And Out-of-Town

Since 1965, the Lyric has been making annual tours throughout Missouri and neighboring states. Starting with the first major tour performance under the auspices of the Missouri State Council in Chillicothe (a community of 10,000 that had requests for over 2,000 tickets for an SRO audience in their 1,000-seat high school auditorium) and later traveling as far afield as South Dakota, Oklahoma, Kansas, and Arkansas with assistance from the Kansas Arts Commission, Great Plains Federation of Arts Councils, or Mid-America Arts Alliance, we have had our share of memorable events.

We have always taken our full company (roughly 100 people counting the cast, chorus, orchestra, and tour crew, which usually travels ahead with the scenery, costumes, and larger musical instruments), so most dates are "runouts" by bus unless the distance requires air travel. On one trip, prior to the oil crisis and when we had dates two days apart in Watertown, South Dakota, and Bartlesville, Oklahoma, we arranged to fly the entire company by charter with a major airline. Unfortunately, we failed to inform the airline that one doesn't serve complimentary drinks on the way to an engagement and food on the return flight.

By the time we were circling the Watertown airport everyone was in a happy mood. Even a snowstorm which suddenly came up as we reached the theater didn't dim the enthusiasm of the audience or the company, and since the storm eased up enough for us to depart after the performance (on our way to warmer Oklahoma), we buffeted our way south with not many food orders demanded!

While we invariably travel with a portable light board and enough instruments for at least adequate lighting effects, we prefer to use the resident lighting system where possible. In fact, where a reasonably new theater exists, the local presentor insists that we use their system. At one tour performance of *Madame Butterfly,* the local instruments did not have gels of the proper colors so our inventive crew attached our gels of a different size to their lights with electrical tape. As the evening progressed and the action as well as the lights grew warmer, a wonderful effect occurred. Just as the eager Pinkerton embraced his Butterfly with the line, "Darkness is falling," gels of various colors began raining down on the stage, and the amorous couple (dodging these noisy and potentially dangerous cherry blossoms) retreated into the doorway of their house for the conclusion of their duet.

Only once in all these years of touring have we forgotten

anything as major as the orchestra parts, when both the librarian and master carpenter thought the other had put the case on the truck. We were doing *The Barber of Seville* in Maryville at Northwest Missouri State University where, fortunately, the music school was able to gather a dozen vocal scores on short notice. While the orchestra parts were being flown up from Kansas City, we did the first act with harpsichord and strings "faking" from vocal scores—delaying the overture until after intermission, when we had the complete orchestra and its music for the remainder of the performance.

Maryville, where we have virtually annual appearances, has been coincidentally the scene of at least two other incidents. It now has a wonderful new theater, but on one earlier visit we actually had several bats join the party in, you guessed it, *Die Fledermaus* at the old auditorium. The other problem occurred when we allowed a leading tenor of the company to fly his own plane to tour engagements since he was on the faculty of Indiana University and commuted. We were touring *Faust* that year and used another tenor for the old Faust in the first scene (thereby instantaneously transforming both the body and voice to young Faust), so our leading tenor/aviator was in the habit of timing his arrival less than half an hour before curtain time. After all, he reasoned, he had the first scene to makeup, dress, and slip into a screened revolving chair.

Unfortunately, we were not aware that the Maryville airport had no lights for night landings until we arrived there. Half the music faculty joined the campus and city police in lining up their car headlights to guide our Faust to his destiny! Shortly after that performance our tenor sold his plane and moved to Kansas City where he is now a member of the faculty at the UMKC Conservatory of Music.

While we take great pride in matching the artistic level of our performances on tour with those at home, certain records are kept by our stage crew when a long run of a production occurs on tour. Most recently, during a tour of *Tosca,* the crew painted a target on the pad where Tosca leaps at the end of the opera, grading her jump every performance like an Olympic event—she got a number of "tens," but our resident Russian Flyman consistently awarded her a "one" or "two"!

Ford-Funds-Feds

Amid the customary headaches of every repertory company is a built-in dilemma with respect to programming, especially with a company espousing the Americanization of opera. For our first five seasons we clung to the standard literature with a caution born of limited financial means while we were concentrating on building an audience for the tried-and-true operas of Verdi, Puccini, Rossini, Mozart, Gounod, et al.

Then, our courage bolstered by a grant from the Ford Foundation, we sallied into the world of Barber, Moore, and Menotti in a special Spring Festival of American Opera in collaboration with the University of Missouri at Kansas City and the Conservatory of Music. The Ford Foundation had helped launch a number of new works at the New York City Center and McNiel Lowry had shown some interest in our fledgling company and its philosophy, although I don't believe anyone from the foundation had been in Kansas City during our actual performance seasons. We, of course, viewed this as an opportunity to move into this exciting new

repertoire and impress the Ford Foundation with our small contribution toward the expansion of American opera into the heart of the country.

From the beginning, this collaborative venture had its problems, and, although the end result was a triumph and helped us develop an audience willing to accept new works (at least to them), half of our opening night was a series of mind-boggling mishaps which created the most embarrassing performance of my career to date!

For this festival, the Lyric was to engage the principal artists, musical staff, directors, and most of the orchestra. The university would supply the theater, technical and design staff, chorus, and supplementary percussion players and stage musicians. The scenery and costumes were built by the Playhouse staff (forerunners of the Missouri Repertory Theater) and were jointly funded by both parties. Since I had worked with Dr. Pat McIlrath at the University Playhouse in the past, I was confident of the artistic level and sense of dedication she always maintained. Our collaboration was a delightful and productive one, but neither of us were prepared for the following series of incidents.

First, the University Chorus was decimated by a last-minute tour of the Heritage Singers that forced us to recruit any student caught lounging on campus as a replacement. Dr. Pat, who was staging *The Devil and Daniel Webster,* agreed to confine all dancing (and indeed any tricky stage movement) to the principal artists and a few experienced extras. I then musically trained the replacement chorus, carefully instructing them to stay out of the way of the action and "never take your eyes off of the conductor."

Then, when we squeezed the enlarged orchestra onto the hydraulic pit of the converted military post theater which served as the University Playhouse, the ancient and overloaded mechanism would not allow us to return the orchestra to floor level (once retracted). I, therefore, requested that the house lights be kept low until I could awkwardly climb out of the pit (unobserved by the audience) at the end of the performance.

Since the orchestra stand lights were attached to a rheostat (which I used to black out the pit during a transformation scene) and the only electrical outlets were at floor level, I cautioned the student electrician (drafted from a Foundations of Theater class) to allow ample extension cords for said rheostat when the pit descended.

Finally, we had cast an experienced character actor in the role of the old fiddler (a speaking part) who was not a musician and who was extremely nervous about miming the playing of a violin and speaking his lines on musical cues.

With all these problems apparently solved, we went into opening night with a full house in the little theater and eager anticipation of sharing our endeavors with our guests from New York. Mac Lowry and Marcia Thompson were flying out for the first weekend when we were alternating performances of *The Devil and Daniel Webster* with *The Medium* and *Vanessa* (which was receiving only its second production). I knew I would see our guests after the opening performance of the double bill, so I strode into the floor level orchestra pit nervously.

First, as the orchestra began the overture and its descent on the hydraulic lift, the curtain also began to descend (rather than rise) revealing rows of lighting instruments. The student crew had grabbed the wrong line! Then, as the pit approached its final resting place, the rheostat became unplugged, blacking out half the orchestra! As I leapt from the podium and managed to lift the rheostat back to the floor level where the outlets were, I saw the entire chorus walk to the edge of the stage—they were "not taking their eyes off the conductor."

After this unnerving opening, our already nervous actor went blank and instead of heralding the entrance of the title role with "Three cheers for Dan'l Webster!", he blurted out, "Let's hear it for Dan'l Boone!" If the artist in the wings could have located a coonskin cap, he would probably have appeared in it. By the end of the performance, I was so mortified and angered that I started for the edge of the pit with murder in my eyes. The student percussion players (seated four feet higher and out of the pit itself) were desperately trying to clear a path for me and accidentally tipped a suspended cymbal into the pit, catching me on the bridge of my nose just as the house lights went to full!

There I was, ingloriously clambering out of the pit and fighting the falling cymbal in full view of the audience! By the time I got into the backstage hallway, I could only laugh at the seemingly unending series of catastrophic events just experienced—so I fled outside the theater to ponder the end of my all-too-brief career. A totally abject stage manager finally found me and persuaded me to return for *The Medium* performance (which was everything the earlier opera wasn't). The Menotti work was, if I may say so, a true piece of exciting musical theater, perhaps because the cast wanted to erase the memory of the preceding work (or maybe they felt they had little else to lose and threw themselves into their parts). Whatever the case, it was a memorable performance for quite different reasons!

As I entered the Green Room after sharing a standing ovation with an exhausted cast, I was greeted by our Ford Foundation guests who congratulated me on the outstanding performance of *The Medium,* while apologizing for having missed *The Devil and Daniel Webster* due to a delayed flight. When asked, "How did the Devil go?", I managed to reply, "Oh, just a typical Lyric performance!" It may have been years later before I found the nerve to tell Mac and Marcia what really happened before they arrived. The subsequent performances, as well as the *Vanessa* which they saw, had none of those problems, and the support of that project by the Ford Foundation encouraged us to continue a policy of including American works in subsequent seasons.

The Martha Baird Rockefeller Fund for Music helped prove a point to some of our colleague companies who were hesitant to do American works because of their losses at the box office. It had been my contention that audiences would accept a limited number of well-produced American works on a seasonal basis, but I had to admit the drop in single ticket sales at those non-standard performances. It also was my opinion that at least some colleagues were using the box office issue to cover the fact that they personally weren't too committed to expanding the repertoire they continued to repeat and which they found much easier to cast with artists readily acceptable to their supporters.

To test this premise, we came up with a "box office support" plan whereby the Lyric would verify its average attendance figure, compare it with the attendance figure at our American work, and bill the MBR Fund for the difference. Thus, they would be underwriting any loss caused by the inclusion of American operas in our season. This project lasted until 1975 when we sold more tickets for *Captain Jinks of the Horse Marines* than we did on average for a season including *La Bohème, The Flying Dutchman, La Périchole,* and *The Marriage of Figaro.* The point had been made, and I was grateful when Maud Brogan assured me that the Lyric didn't owe MBR box office support for the standard works!

By this time, the National Endowment for the Arts had been authorized, and the American Symphony Orchestra League was representing that art form nationally. Glenn Ross (who was famous for "marketing" opera throughout the Pacific Northwest and had been quite successful in working with his local and state governments as well as the area federal representatives) invited about a dozen opera companies to a meeting in Seattle. Glenn convinced us that there was a need for a unified voice for opera in America and we needed to become more informed about each other's experiences with our state and regional arts councils. Out of that first informal meeting came the organization and establishment of Opera America (the growth of which has affected all of us in the field) but, except for several important artswide programs still being assisted by the Ford Foundation, this ended most of those individual pilot projects which helped us through our formative years.

Co-Opera

I don't mean to imply that we at the Lyric (or many of our colleagues around the country) were working in a vacuum or were unaware of what others were accomplishing. There was, however, a resemblance to the colonies prior to the First Continental Congress among the few regional opera-producing organizations (with the Metropolitan Opera being viewed by too many of us as King George) before the formation of Opera America. In fact, the old adage that we had better hang together lest we all hang separately was mentioned more than once at the Seattle meeting. Of the Big Four (the Metropolitan, San Francisco, Chicago Lyric, and New York City Opera), only San Francisco was represented at the meeting. Since we couldn't expect any organization purporting to represent opera throughout the country to have national credibility without these prestigious companies, we wanted them involved.

Because Kurt Adler, General Director of the San Francisco Opera, was highly respected by Carol Fox of the Chicago Lyric and I had a close personal friend in Carol's Assistant

Manager Ardis Krainik (now the General Manager there), we were assigned the task of involving Carol in our plans. We all felt that Carol and Kurt together had the best chance of convincing Sir Rudolf Bing of the necessity of our all hanging together, which, of course, they eventually did and Opera America became truly that unified voice.

To illustrate the general atmosphere surrounding the art form at that time, almost half of those representing the 20 companies that assembled to organize Opera America formally at a subsequent session at Lincoln Center had never sat down together before. Since we were still awaiting the Met's reply to our invitation, the standing joke was, "A well-placed bomb from the adjacent building would leave the Metropolitan as the sole professional opera company in the U.S.!" I hasten to add that Sir Rudolf dramatically entered our meeting, put our fears to rest by assuring us the support of the Met's membership, and introduced his recently named successor, Geran Gentile.

Prior to this historic occasion, the Metropolitan Opera had for some years maintained little direct contact with other opera-producing organizations, although its national council members were individually involved with many of our companies and the Central Opera Service through the superhuman efforts of Maria Rich had functioned as an important resource library. Many of us had, as professional members of the council, taken part in the district and regional auditions, and a few of us followed with great interest the development of the Metropolitan Opera Studio, created by John Gutman and headed by Bill Nix. Mr. Gutman had been especially helpful to young American artists and on many occasions sent those he felt were ready for their first *Tosca* or *Butterfly* to the Lyric. He felt that our company could offer these especially promising young people, who were often beyond the studio level but not yet ready to face New York reviewers in roles more demanding than the fourth Valkyrie or second villager, a rare experience for that time. A fairly extensive rehearsal period with experienced stage directors and coaches, a rotating repertoire system allowing an artist the time needed to carefully put the role into the voice, and a reasonably sized theater with good acoustics in which to do all this were to Mr. Gutman much better answers to the needs of developing artists than those offered in Europe. We, in turn, had the advantage of Mr. Gutman's experience and contacts in locating these promising young artists.

Two of our major supporters, Louis Sosland, Chairman of the Board, and Dr. Revis Lewis, long-time friend of Francis Robinson of the Met staff, were active in the national council. They decided to show support for the Annual National Auditions Finals by offering the Sosland/Lewis Award to one of the finalists on the stage of the Metropolitan. This award included a contract with the Lyric Opera in

Kansas City. Since our own repertoire and an appropriate role would have to be chosen for our forthcoming season, it was agreed that Mr. Gutman and I would select one of the finalists and jointly choose his or her debut role. To my knowledge, this was the first time any regional company had taken an official stance in support of the auditions with this kind of commitment.

After Sir Rudolf introduced Mr. Gentile to us at that meeting in New York, I was surprised when Mr. Gentile asked "Which of you is from the Kansas City Opera?" At his request, I followed him into the hall for a brief conversation. He had noticed that few companies had indicated a desire to support the auditions (as we had with the prize and contract), already knew of the cooperation we had enjoyed with John Gutman, and wished to establish closer working relationships with regional companies similar to ours. His visit that spring was a brief (and busy) one, so he suggested that I meet with him upon his return in the fall. His experience with European houses (where singers' careers were followed closely as they advanced from Bielefeld and Frankfurt to Munich and Berlin) suggested the need for a "farm system" in our country which could benefit regional companies and the Met. It would also create an atmosphere conducive to the growth of American artists in an orderly fashion. I have often wondered what might have happened had he lived to pursue that idea.

As Opera America became a more active organization, many of us with similar formats and goals began working together on various committees. Shared productions are now becoming accepted, but in the early days of our organization we were just beginning to identify our common needs, strengths, and weaknesses.

While serving on committees dealing with national auditions, English translations, and the development of apprentice programs, Wesley Balk of the Minnesota Opera, David Lloyd of the Lake George Opera Festival, and I decided to collaborate. Co-Opera was more than an exchange of scenery, it was a method of combining the strengths of three companies of similar ideals but geographically separated and producing at different times of the year. By sharing production concepts, artistic staffs, and casting (as well as pooling rehearsal time), we felt we could offer more attractive engagements to artists, improve our individual offerings, and effect savings in our growing budgets. The collaboration was an enjoyable one, although it was cut short by the incompatibility of our respective theaters at the time. I still feel the concept a valid one. In a sense, Co-Opera does still function even though some of the originators have moved on to other positions. Last season we joined the Minnesota Opera in producing *Where the Wild Things Are,* and its companion piece was designed by Maurice Sendak as a joint venture with Lake George.

RECAPITULATION

Festival Fun and Games

For the past 11 years, we have been producing an annual festival at Thespian Hall in Boonville, Missouri, the Missouri River Festival of the Arts. Presented under the auspices of the Friends of Historic Boonville, this has become an example of cooperative involvement in the arts by the citizens of a small, but historic, community. Inspired by the generosity of a family foundation with a genuine love of the arts and historical preservation and assisted by funding from a state arts council that considers it a model of community arts programming which serves an ever-expanding out-state area, Boonville has become a meeting ground for artists and patrons on an unusually personal level.

The Missouri River Festival started somewhat accidentally but has proved to be a greatly anticipated annual event of regional importance. It illustrates, probably more than any other example in this book, the acceptance of and involvement in opera-theater as an indigenous art form by sometimes relatively inexperienced but open-minded, friendly, and generally inquisitive (as well as outspoken) supporters of the arts in Mid-America.

When our company moved downtown and finally acquired its year-round home, I asked R. Crosby Kemper, whose foundation had recently sponsored a production of *The Flying Dutchman,* to assist us in the refurbishing of the Capri Theatre. In our conversation, Mr. Kemper casually mentioned that his foundation had recently helped the Friends of Historic Boonville save Thespian Hall and that they were working on a restoration of the historic theater. He felt that this once prominent hall should become again a home for arts activity.

On the following weekend, I visited Boonville and was shown the hall and most of the town by several members of the historical society. I had, of course, often driven through Boonville for years (generally en route to Columbia or St. Louis) but was unprepared for the friendly and informative visit awaiting me. Boonville, like a number of Missouri River towns, had a large number of antebellum homes but, unlike most other towns, had Thespian Hall. It had been built in 1850 as a town hall and meeting place but was converted into the Stephens Opera House in the 1870s after serving as a temporary hospital during a Civil War battle. Incidentally, since Boonville is located in a section of the state called "Little Dixie," some of its citizens still refer to that conflict as the War for Southern Independence. As a matter of fact, when the local festival chorus first performed "The Battle

Hymn of the Republic" with the festival orchestra, it was immediately followed by "Dixie" (complete with miniature Rebel flags).

In discovering the origins of this acoustically marvelous hall with members of the Friends of Historic Boonville, I discovered why this community was once reputed to be the cultural center of the state. It seems that Boonville was approximately half-way between St. Louis and St. Joseph (the starting point for the Oregon Trail as Independence was for the Santa Fe Trail) so artists bound for Central City, Colorado, and points west often stopped in Boonville to appear at Thespian Hall. When refurbishing the stage area and restoring a pit in the theater, we discovered evidence of the appearances of such artists as Edwin Booth and Jenny Lind during the glory days of the old hall.

In an effort to involve an unsuspecting community in an arts festival suddenly thrust upon it (does this sound familiar?), the small committee, led by a friend of Mr. Kemper who was active in the restoration of the state's Governor's Mansion, decided to surround the festival performances with sporting events, cast parties, joint company and patrons' picnics, etc. In these efforts to make both the visiting artists and local volunteers more comfortable with each other, we found ourselves with another family situation which has grown ever more close over the years.

We now have a golf tournament (usually won by a team

composed of a stagehand, one of the singers or Lyric staff members, and several of the local patrons). The invitational tennis tournament invariably has winners from both Boonville and the visiting artists, and it's every man for himself in the Run for the Arts! The only time sides are taken is in the challenge of a volleyball game at the annual picnic, and even there we usually have at least one capsized canoe containing festival patrons, artists, and assorted children and dogs—all happily splashing together.

By the way, we do also present two opera performances (ranging from Mozart to Puccini), concerts by the Kansas City Symphony and other guest recitalists, dance companies, etc., during this two week time of fun and games. The artists have rediscovered old-fashioned milkshakes at the corner drugstore, outfitted themselves with boots at a sale timed to coincide with the festival, and look forward to eating Missouri River catfish each year. The local supporters have acted as "supers" on stage, adopted everyone from the stage crew to the chorus, and enjoy lying around their swimming pools with all of us as members of the family. The Missouri River Festival has become a "Same Time Next Year" love affair in the middle of the "Show Me" state!

Repertoire–Who Done It!

No chronicle of experiences would be complete without a compilation of the repertoire presented by the Lyric Opera of Kansas City during the past 30 seasons and a list of company members who contributed so much to the growth of the company. A decade ago, the late Honorary Chairman of our Board, Henry C. Haskell, wrote "20th Anniversary Waltz" in which he included those listings. Henry also covered much of the material which makes up this chronicle in a much more concise and orderly manner than I could achieve, so I have merely updated his listings and plagiarized (on more than one occasion) Henry's article. That's just one more debt the Lyric (and I personally) owe one of the founders and most eloquent original spokesmen for the principles upon which our company is based.

Repertoire of the Lyric Opera of Kansas City
(1958-59 through 1987-88)

Barber: *Vanessa* (1963, 1965, 1979)
Beeson: *The Sweet Bye and Bye* (1973)
Captain Jinks of the Horse Marines (1975)

Bernstein:	*Candide* (1984)
Beethoven:	*Fidelio* (1981, 1983)
Bizet:	*Carmen* (1959, 1968, 1979)
Blitzstein:	*Regina* (1981)
Donizetti:	*Don Pasquale* (1960, 1966)
	Elixir of Love (1963, 1968, 1980)
	Lucia di Lammermoor (1981)
	Daughter of the Regiment (1987)
Flotow:	*Martha* (1985)
Floyd:	*Of Mice and Men* (1970)
	Susannah (1977)
Giannini:	*The Taming of the Shrew* (1969, 1971)
Giordano:	*Andrea Chénier* (1962, 1968, 1976)
Gounod:	*Faust* (1962, 1966, 1978, 1985)
Hoiby:	*The Tempest* (1987)
Kander:	*The Happy Time* (1982)
Knussen:	*Where the Wild Things Are* (1986)
Lehár:	*The Merry Widow* (1981)
Leoncavallo:	*Pagliacci* (1958, 1970)
Mascagni:	*Cavalleria Rusticana* (1961, 1970)
Massenet:	*Manon* (1980)
Menotti:	*The Medium* (1963, 1964, 1978)
	The Saint of Bleecker Street (1972)
Moore:	*The Ballad of Baby Doe* (1976, 1982)
	The Devil and Daniel Webster (1963)
Mozart:	*Abduction from the Seraglio* (1958, 1972)
	Cosi Fan Tutte (1962, 1984)
	Don Giovanni (1960, 1967, 1979)
	The Goose from Cairo (1981, 1986)
	The Magic Flute (1974)
	The Marriage of Figaro (1961, 1964, 1970, 1975, 1977, 1987)
Nicolai:	*The Merry Wives of Windsor* (1963)
Offenbach:	*La Périchole* (1973, 1975, 1983)
	Christopher Columbus (1979)

	La Belle Hélène (1980)
	Tales of Hoffmann (1965, 1969, 1977)
Orff:	*Die Kluge* (1971, 1978)
Pergolesi:	*La Serva Padrona* (1958)
Puccini:	*La Bohème* (1958, 1961, 1964, 1969, 1982)
	Tosca (1959, 1963, 1967, 1973, 1975, 1986)
	Madame Butterfly (1960, 1965, 1971, 1980, 1987)
	Gianni Schicchi (1961, 1964, 1971)
	Girl of the Golden West (1978)
	Turandot (1984)
Rossini:	*Barber of Seville* (1959, 1962, 1967, 1971, 1976, 1982)
	La Cenerentola (1983)
	The Italian in Algiers (1981)
Sondheim:	*Sweeney Todd* (1985)
Sousa:	*The Free Lance* (1980)
J. Strauss:	*Die Fledermaus* (1974, 1987)
R. Strauss:	*Ariadne Auf Naxos* (1966, 1978)
	Der Rosenkavalier (1987)
Sullivan:	*The Pirates of Penzance* (1976, 1986)
	H.M.S. Pinafore (1978)
	Iolanthe (1979)
	The Mikado (1977, 1984)
	The Yeomen of the Guard (1963, 1972)
Susa:	*Transformations* (1974)
Thomson:	*The Mother of Us All* (1982)
Verdi:	*Aida* (1972, 1977)
	Masked Ball (1967, 1985)
	Rigoletto (1959, 1964, 1969, 1982)
	La Traviata (1960, 1965, 1974, 1984)
	Il Trovatore (1966, 1983)
	Forza Del Destino (1961)
	Otello (1958, 1963, 1970)
	Falstaff (1986)

Wagner: *The Flying Dutchman* (1973, 1975)
Der Ring des Nibelungen, Scenes (1982)
Ward: *The Crucible* (1968, 1986)
Weill: *The Threepenny Opera* (1985)

The Lyric on Tour

1965 – *Madame Butterfly*
1966 – *Faust*
1967 – *The Barber of Seville*
1968 – *Elixir of Love*
1969 – *La Bohème*
1970 – *The Marriage of Figaro*
1971 – *Madame Butterfly*
1972 – *The Yeomen of the Guard*
1973 – Lyric in Concert
1974 – Lyric in Concert
1975 – Lyric in Concert
1976 – *The Barber of Seville*
1977 – *The Marriage of Figaro*
1978 – *The Medium* and *Die Kluge*
    H.M.S. Pinafore
1979 – *Don Giovanni*
1980 – *Elixir of Love*
1981 – *The Italian in Algiers*
1982 – *Rigoletto*
1983 – *La Périchole*
1984 – *Cosi Fan Tutte*
    The Mikado
1985 – *Faust*
1986 – *Tosca*
    The Pirates of Penzance
1987 – *The Marriage of Figaro*

Operas produced: 73
Performances at home and on the road: 995

The Company

Over the last 30 years many talented young artists have performed with the Lyric. Some began their professional careers with us, others gained their first experience in major roles on our stage. A few have told us they might not have continued except for the opportunity provided by this house. We are proud of all of them. The names that follow constitute merely a random sampling and include a number who were already launched in their careers when they came to us. The list could easily be extended, but I believe it is fairly representative.

Judith Anthony	Dorothy Danner
Karen Beardsley	Harry Danner
William Beck	William Dansby
Brenda Boozer	Barbara Davis
Phillip Bologna	J. B. Davis
Evan Bortnick	Roseanne del George
Gene Bullard	Judith dePaul
Jane Bunnell	Judith Dickinson
Barry Busse	John Robert Dunlap
June Card	Marc Embree
Catherine Christiansen	David Evitts
Dorothy Cole	Edward Evanko
Elaine Cormany	Robert Ferrier
Dorothy Coulter	Mildred Fling
Claudia Cummings	Harlan Foss
Davis Cunningham	Kathleen Fogarty
Kay Creed	Carroll Freeman
Sharon Daniels	Kathryn Gamberoni
John Davies	Gary Glaze
Edith Davis	Eugene Green

Kay Griffel
Helene Guilet
Roberta Gumbel
Gail Hadani
Richard Halverson
Lowell Harris
Leslie Herrington
Joanne Highley
Ronald Highley
David Holloway
Walter Hook
Ann Irving
Rosemary Jackson
Carolyn James
Gwendolyn James
Robert Jones
Ruby Jones
William Justus
Marlena Kleinman
Richard Knoll
Stanley Kolk
William Ledbetter
Joanna Levy
George Livings
George Massey
William McDonald
Adair McGowen
Spiro Malas
Cynthia Miller
Cynthia Munzer
Joan Moynagh

Thomas Palmer
Joan Patenaude
Abe Polakoff
Kay Paschal
Henry Price
William Powers
Sam Resnick
Michael Reiley
Dean Rhodus
Francesca Roberto
Noelle Rogers
Cynthia Rose
James Schwisow
Nancy Shade
Vernon Shinall
Jerold Siena
Alma Jean Smith
Roy Samuelson
Catherine Stapleton
Brian Steele
Dan Sullivan
Nolan Van Way
Elizabeth Volkman
Diana Walker
Andrew Wentzel
Stanley Wexler
Carol Wilcox
Gran Wilson
Robert Williams
Karen Yarmat

Among our Conductors:

Philip Brunelle
Michael Charry
Rick Fanning
Hal France
Istvan Gladies
George Lawner

Paulette Haupt-Nolen
Russell Patterson
Jeffrey Powell
Byron Dean Ryan
Rudolf Fellner

Among our Designers:

Keith Brumley
Patton Campbell
Robert E. Darling
John Ezell
Christiana Giannini
James Gohl
Robert Israel

Frederick James
James Joy
Harold Peter
G. Philippe de Rosier
Martin Ross
Maurice Sendak

Among our Stage Directors:

Ross Allen
Patrick Bakman
Wesley Balk
Roger Brunyate
Frank Corsaro
Francis Cullinan
James di Blasis
Robert E. Darling
Jack Eddleman

David Hicks
James Luckas
Christopher Mattaliano
Patricia McIlrath
Francis Rizzo
Christian Smith
Ian Strasfogel
Nicholas Muni
J. Morton Walker

Quo Vadis—Auf English

In earlier chapters of this view of the first 30 years of what I believe is a continuing experiment (which originally proposed to transplant the then almost universally accepted European opera-theater pattern to a more or less typical American setting), I referred to some of my experiences while studying and working abroad. The basis of that experiment was an attempt to produce opera in English as theater and on a repertory basis. The use of the language most commonly utilized by the great majority of our potential audiences was only a part, albeit a vital one, of attracting those audiences to opera-theater. For centuries in Europe (actually since the Camerata first attempted to recapture a form of Greek theater), opera had been considered much more than a purely musical entertainment. Composers, often inspired by theatrical or literary works and in some cases their own political beliefs, used this multifaceted art form as a forum to comment on life as they saw it or promote their philosophies. Only by direct and instantaneous communication is that ideally possible.

Once opera became more than an evening's diversion for court theaters, it became an indigenous part of the social, cultural, and even political life of every country in Europe but always was performed in the language of the people there. After years of being exposed to a steady diet of Verdi in German, Strauss in Italian, and Wagner in French (not to mention all of them in Swedish), audiences all over Europe (who are generally a bit more multilingual than we) can now accept original language performances by international casts. I do suspect, however, their familiarity with the works is due to an understanding derived from a lifetime of repeated exposure in their own language.

Arguments over translations in opera have raged for years. Artists, who perform the same roles in many languages, are often reluctant to do so, even though they are striving for theatrically persuasive interpretations as well as vocal ones. Phyllis Curtin, whose reputation as a consummate singing-actress, is undisputed, once related to me a most telling incident. It seems that after a performance in English, enhanced I am sure with all of her musical artistry and stage technique, Phyllis was approached by a member of the audience who said: "My, you were wonderful, but I wish you hadn't sung in English. It forced me to try to follow what was going on, and I like to just sit back and let the music wash over me!" The undoubtedly exhausted, but always gracious, artist replied, "But my dear, Mozart didn't write music to bathe in!" It is true that Mozart composed, on commission, a number of magnificent divertimenti and serenades, which were probably first heard as dinner or party entertainments, but his operas range from settings of Beaumarche satires on social conditions to Masonic statements, which all require understandable characterizations.

Probably the most often stated arguments against doing opera in translation are that it either fails to support the composer's intent or it just doesn't sound right (meaning it doesn't sound the same to one who is accustomed to hearing certain sounds on certain notes). There is no answer to the latter statement, which has little to do with the concept of opera as a communicative art form. As to the more serious argument, let us look to the composer's intent. Take, for example, Giuseppe Verdi, considered by most to be the utmost nationalist of Italian composers.

At the premiere of *Don Carlo,* which was done in France and for which the management wished to perform in Italian with leading artists imported from his native Italy, Verdi sued to force the use of French, explaining that he wrote his operas for the people, not for critics or producers, and wished his works done in a manner which allowed the people to understand them. He won and so did, I suspect, the public!

I have given up arguing with those who use pure "authenticity" as the justification for the original language production. I merely agree that anyone who insists on reading Tolstoy in the original Russian, wouldn't be caught dead at a Molière play unless it were in the original French, and actually prefers untranslated foreign films certainly has the right to demand his "musical theater" in its original form. When we as a nation have reached that cultural state, none of us will need to demystify opera for our potential audiences. Until then, one fact remains virtually unanswerable: in countries where opera was first introduced and had a chance to be understood as a theatrical as well as musical form, it has enjoyed great popularity. Meanwhile, in those countries where it has been presented primarily in the original language, opera has remained of relatively limited appeal.

Much has been made in recent years of the use of subtitles, "sur-titles," or "sur-caps" as a method of breaking the communication barrier. This innovation, adapted from a more understandable use on film and television, has undoubtedly at least kept audiences somewhat aware of the story line (if slightly less aware of the histrionic abilities of the performers) and is reputed to be attracting larger audiences to opera houses. Even if the latter is true, I consider it a trade-off that doesn't address the issue of involvement or quality of the experience. To miss those subtle theatrical gestures which artists spend a lifetime achieving while having one's attention drawn to projected text (often abridged) creates less involvement in a total experience. Why not just stay home with your complete libretto and a note perfect musical performance sung by the incomparable Renata Milanov in enhanced digital stereo? You can even command instant encores of your favorite arias and insert your own intermissions to refresh your scotch and soda—all while attired in your smoking jacket and lounging in your favorite chair. Cultured it may be, but immersed in all the elements of great musical theater it ain't!

Presenting live performances of opera in English for these nigh on to 30 years has given us more than a few opportunities for improvising texts (one does have that problem in other languages more than you might suspect). I witnessed quite a few instances in Germany, for example, where unsuspecting young *auslanders* were coached by their more experienced resident colleagues in the subtleties of singing German in translation—the result of which was surprising to say the least. Even the best of intentions can often leave an audience in temporary shock. We were doing Shakespeare's *Otello,* set gloriously by Verdi to Boito's admirable adaptation, and were utilizing the original Shakespeare text whenever possible. This included Emilia's cry upon discovering Desdemona's lifeless body, "Help, help, the Moor has murdered my mistress!" With such alliteration in the text, is it any wonder we all heard a slightly confused mezzo-soprano voice suddenly utter, "Help, help, the murderer has Moored my mistress!" When the startled audience finally stopped laughing, I realized one good thing had occurred: they all were involved in the performance. The play was the thing! I think both Shakespeare and Verdi would have agreed.

Afterword (A Continuing Coda)

Today in the United States there exist more than 100 resident professional opera companies, many offering coherent annual seasons. This has been an update on the first 30 years of one such enterprise.

Our original manifesto gathers dust in our office files. We blow the cobwebs off this credo occasionally (also printing it as part of periodic updates) as a reminder that the Lyric continues to be an ongoing experiment dedicated to its basic principles. The Lyric was launched at a propitious moment and allowed to develop at its own pace without distorting our purpose or rushing into a premature expansion. Those preconditions would not be easy to duplicate today, and while other performing arts organizations in our area have experienced dramatic fluctuations, our company has maintained a steady growth both artistically and in acceptance by an increasingly involved public. After three decades, our experience indicates that opera-theater performed in English by well-trained young artists constitutes an exceptionally attractive form of entertainment for an American community. We stand persuaded that, given certain minimal preconditions, this art will speak for itself to any American audience.

The Lyric Opera of Kansas City's reputation was not built on stars, imported or otherwise, and we like to think we have never tried to market opera by comparison by resorting to the use of box-office names to lend the enchantment of far-away places to our productions. Our audiences attend in formal wear or shirtsleeves, as they wish. We also like to think that our audiences have as much fun at our performances as they do at our most successful (and most important) galas, chocolate festivals, and other social events.

Our original goals (and dreams for the acceptance of opera-theater) have never changed but at least one result in our company has been surprising. Like so many of my young colleagues when we started out 30 years ago, I thought that producing opera as theater in English, with well-rehearsed, talented artists, and conscious of the theatrical involvement a relatively unexposed audience could experience would naturally, and easily, attract the great mass of Americans just waiting for the opportunity to discover us. Instead, I now realize that, as P. T. Barnum and Sol Hurok certainly knew, one need still only announce the limited appearance of a Pavarotti or Domingo and thousands will materialize for that event, sung in any language and rehearsed or not. What I am delighted to discover is that we have developed a most knowledgeable and loyal audience throughout our region who have truly become imbued with a sense of involvement and participation, not just observation.

These open-minded, and sometimes quite outspoken, converts to opera as theater can often be heard in animated discussions during an intermission at the Lyric concerning the values they perceive at the performance. Not how Stephanie Singspiel handled a certain phrase compared to last season's favorite Renata Rallentando (as many opera buffs do throughout the world), but rather holding forth with personal feelings about a convincingly portrayed Mimi, the effectiveness of scenic and lighting design in capturing the attempted style of that production, or even what philosophical impact Wagner was striving to achieve (and did we help him to do so). That's a sign of true involvement.

When it all started 30 years ago, we asked ourselves, "Would Kansas City accept opera presented in so unorthodox a manner by the then prevailing national standards—without stars or spectacular stage investitures?" Many friends told us it couldn't be done. We think we have been proving them wrong ever since. In another 30 years we may know for sure.